Students

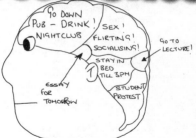

GO DOWN PUB - DRINK!
NIGHTCLUB
SEX!
FLIRTING!
SOCIALISING!
GO TO LECTURE!
STAY IN BED TILL 3PM
ESSAY FOR TOMORROW
STUDENT PROTEST

Charlotte Hathaway

Crombie Jardine
PUBLISHING LIMITED

13 Nonsuch Walk, Cheam, Surrey, SM2 7LG
www.crombiejardine.com

Published by Crombie Jardine Publishing Limited
First edition, 2005

Copyright © 2005,
Crombie Jardine Publishing Limited

ISBN 1-905102-26-7

Written by Charlotte Hathaway
Cartoons by Helen West
Designed by www.glensaville.com
Printed & bound in the United Kingdom by
William Clowes Ltd, Beccles, Suffolk

Dedicated to all students at Edinburgh University, as it is clearly the best.

With many thanks to all of my contributors, especially Pete Lee, Martin Banwell, and Natalie Farmer.

CONTENTS

INTRODUCTION

Here is a guide to The Student – that inherently useless proportion of the population that nonetheless requires a vast amount of government funding and acts as though it has the right to an opinion, just because it is 'educated'.

Whether you are one, have been one or would cross the road to avoid one, read on to find out more about this fascinating species!

So what is the point of university? This is a very debated topic, and a question asked by many. There are countless theories and here are just a few hypotheses given by students I interviewed:

1. 'To get laid as many times as humanly possible, stocking up on sex before the kids arrive and marriage takes its toll.'

2. 'To demand discounts in every shop you go into.'

3. 'To find more and more dates in the calendar that are a cause for celebration and heavy drinking.'

4. 'To keep the people who make signs, traffic cones and shopping trolleys in business by ensuring that there is always a shortage.'

5. 'To piss off the locals.'

6. 'To put off the real world for another 3 years (or 4 if you are a student in Scotland).'

7. 'To see how close you can get to a deadline before starting any work.'

8. 'To put Communism into practice (living in halls etc, sharing food,

alcohol, underwear, drugs, blood...
money from the government).'

9. 'To meet new people, get away
from your parents, grow some
balls, and prepare yourself
for the cruel world that you
are about to have to fend for
yourself in.'

10. 'To get onto the next rung of the
ladder of life as perceived by
middle Britain.'

Generally speaking, most people would agree that it is not to watch Neighbours twice a day or to find out once and for all how long you can go without clean clothes.

According to the 1950s sociological theory behind a non-vocational degree, the point of university is 'to foster a sense of cognitive rationality'. But nowadays many people would argue that there is little evidence to support the point of going to university (at least no point that the Government could justify in legislative wording) and what is learned will be forgotten when

the student graduates, stops drinking,
and wakes from a three-year daze
wondering what the hell happened.
Hurray for students!

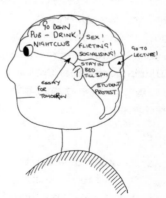

STUDENT SPOTTING

WHERE TO FIND THEM

It is a common misconception that students actually spend most of their time in university, and therefore probably foolish to begin your search there. For a more effective search, the following places should be explored first:

The pub

This seems rather obvious, but many students do tend to be unimaginative and live up to their stereotype. They can be found here at any time of the day during opening hours, depending on how early they have managed to get out of bed.

The university library

In normal circumstances this would be an odd place to go looking for students. But in the week before exams this is a likely location: the students have suddenly realised that they are not infallible and can get kicked out of uni when it becomes apparent through the examination system that they have done sod all throughout the year.

The supermarket

This is a good student-spotting place, either in the middle of the night (when all the cheap stuff is being sold off), or in the middle of the day (see the reduced isle). Do not underestimate the power of the freezer-section.

Grassy areas

In the summer months, students will be out in their droves, trying to sunbathe. As the sun invariably only shines during exam time, excuses to justify being outdoors will include the common buzzwords of 'revision', 'procrastination', and 'therapeutic relaxation'.

Eating places

For the more pretentious/wealthy students (typically Yahs and Hippies), a smoothie shop is a good bet. For the more classic student, cheap curry houses and all-you-can-eat Chinese are popular.

Clothes shops

All students like to buy clothes. A student has an image of stylish poverty to maintain. Regularly visited are charity shops and places like Primark or T.K.Maxx.

Street corners waiting to 'pick up'

This is a term for meeting one's dealer, and as students of course all smoke weed, pop pills, and have fun with mushrooms, you are guaranteed to get lucky and come across a good few.

Clubs on Wednesday nights

Sensible people realise that they can make a lot of money out of students as most care little for their studies and will be out clubbing and drinking until the small hours on week nights.

If you are fortunate enough to live in a city with a campus university located away from the centre, you may be spared the influx of students in many of these places as the student is too lazy to go into town. However they do find ways of making it to the most inconvenient places, so beware!

TIPS FOR BLENDING IN AS A STUDENT

To blend in with the student crowd, I recommend the following:

1. Do not wash for at least a week, and allow hair to settle into that unbrushed-just-got-out-of-bed shape.

2. Try not to sleep for a couple of nights, ensuring that you partake in heavy drinking on at least one of these nights for maximum hangover-appearance and puffy-eye effect.

3. Adopt an expression of general nonchalance and 'I am far cooler than mere mortal non-students can comprehend because I have a Life'.

4. Know a lot of big and clever words, but make sure you use them in slightly suspect contexts for fear people think you actually know what you're talking about.

5. Talk loudly and obnoxiously about how many hot people you shagged this week, don't give details of their names because if

you are a real student you either
a) don't remember their names,
or b) the people are fictional.

6. Develop some weird slang,
obscure in-jokes and private
codes, such as 'wds40...IQZ...
monkey...8748ppl...omg!!'.

7. Take up 'partying' and declare
as frequently as possible that
you and your friends are 'mental'.
For example, before an exam
make sure that you stay out
clubbin' until 3am, and turn up
to the exam still drunk. This will

make you a true 'party animal'.

8. Tell everybody how stoned you got last Glastonbury and ended up with a cat, two sheep, and a small vole sleeping in your tent with you, before thinking it would be a fun idea to take mushrooms, go for a swim in the mud, and join a nudist hippy commune.

9. Adopt these mottos: 'A job worth doing is worth being done by someone else', 'If you want the job done properly, give me a raise', 'If no-one

misses it, it ain't theft'.

10. And lastly, bear in mind at all
    times that university is a chance
    for everybody, even socially
    inept weirdoes, to get laid at
    least once before they die.

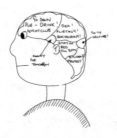

GLOSSARY OF TERMS

Students are known for creating and using to extremes ridiculous abbreviations and slang. Here are a few examples to help you understand what they are saying:

To get the munchies = To be inexplicably hungry.

To be skint = To have no money.

The Fear = The crushing realisation that exams are in a few days and you don't know shit.

Tropospheric pernicious redolence = Particularly vile smelling fart.

To skive = To miss a lecture/tutorial in order to do something far more worthwhile like sleep, drink, watch TV.

Minging/mingin' = Something or someone highly undesirable and aesthetically displeasing. E.g. Urg, he's well mingin'.

Pants = Somewhat disappointing and inadequate.

Jizz = Sperm.

Mawing = Eating.

To doss about = To do very little of any use or consequence.

Morning lecture = Lie-in.

Afternoon lecture = Trip to the shops/drinking session.

Tutorial/seminar = Waste of time/ drinking session.

Work = What you do when you have no money to spend on drugs or go drinking/clubbing with.

'Do you want to go to the pub for

a pint?' = 'Do you want to go out and spend everything that happens to be in your wallet on whatever drinks promotion the bar is running tonight?'

'Sorry Mum, I can't, I've got soooo much work to do. I've got, like, five essays, all due tomorrow, and exams all next week.' = 'I shall decline your invitation as I cannot be bothered to even give it thought.'

'Sorry, can't, skint, man.' = 'I would rather die than spend my valuable drinking cash on doing that with you, or buying that from/for you.'

'Cool beans!' = 'That sounds delightful!'

'Lacking inspiration due to exam stress.' = 'I can't be bothered to work out what you are asking me to think about just now, and I probably won't give it any thought at a later date either.'

SPARE TIME ACTIVITIES

University life isn't all work and no play, a vast range of activities are provided to make sure that a student gets the most out of their university experience...

Top 10 student leisure pursuits

1. Drinking

It cannot be emphasised enough how stereotypical students are in their pursuit of this pastime.

2. Daytime TV

Few things are more stimulating for students than quality broadcasting such as Neighbours, and Judge Judy.

3. Societies

Societies are generally just an excuse for a piss-up, from the glaringly obvious such as the 'Tennants Appreciation Society' to the more subtle, such as 'Theology Soc.'.

4. Making full use of uni free contraceptives

Students like to have sex. And lots of it. This can be done anywhere, at any time, with anybody.

5. Internet

With free Internet access for most students, uni network black-markets develop (where movies and albums are pirated and passed between those savvy enough with technology to manage it).

6. Music

As everybody knows, it is very cool to be in a band. It is even

cooler to piss off your neighbours
by holding a 'band practice'
(consisting of the abuse of
instruments under the influence of
alcohol and narcotics) in your flat.

7. Spending the student loan

If not spent on alcohol, as a rule the
student loan must be spent on silly
things like a giant furry pink sofa,
a novelty drinks fridge, or a mobile
phone complete with camera, mp3
player, and herb garden that will do
your shopping for you.

8. Late-night philosophy

Students like to think they're very deep and intellectual, and therefore have lengthy discussions to this tune full of long words and terminology, aided by philosophical substances such as weed.

9. Complaining

Students feel very hard-done-by and like to bitch among themselves about how badly they are treated by the university, the Government, their tutor, and their significant other. They also like to complain about how much work they get, the price of weed, the amount of loan they get, their parents, anything else under the sun.

10. Sport

Yes, some students *do* do this, usually when all other methods to attract the opposite sex and secure a shag have failed and 'shaping up' becomes the last resort of the desperate.

Top 10 weird university societies

1. Boris Johnson
   Appreciation Society
   York

2. Rock, Paper, Scissors Society
   Bath

3. Basil Brush Society
   Strathclyde

4. Macintosh Users Society
   Edinburgh

5. Jedi Society
   Leicester

6. Tea Drinking Society
   Sheffield

7. Neighbours Society
   Nottingham

8. Assassin's Guild
   Cambridge

9. Surrey Gurners (a society
   for gurning!)
   Surrey

10. Absinthe Dunelm (promoting the
    enjoyment of Absinthe)
    Durham

LIVING CONDITIONS

HYDRATION

A student cannot live up to its stereotype without drinking. Alcohol preferably. Here is a list of a student's favourites:

Top 10 student drinks

1. Cheap lager: Carling (England/ Wales), Tennants Lager (Scotland/ N. Ireland)

2. Guinness (it's a meal in itself, useful for a starving student

to bear in mind)

3. Snakebite

4. £1 shots and Vodka Redbull (when on offer), any 2 for 1 student offer

5. Cheap Lidl's £2.99-a-bottle wine (although much of this must be consumed as the alcohol content is negligible)

6. VK bottles

7. Lambrusco (just that little bit cheaper than Lambrini)

8. 3-litre bottles of White Lightning

9. Own brand spirits

10. Water from the tap (only when truly skint, or trying to sober up – Heaven forbid)

N.B. To keep a happy student, keep it well-watered.

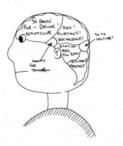

NUTRITION

To be a successful student and not starve, one must realize the value of one's freezer-section. And the infinite use of a microwave. You know you're a student when you find yourself paying for a packet of crisps by Switch.

Top 10 student meals

1. Lidl's '3 for 99p' pizzas

2. Potato waffles – they go with *anything*

3. Ye olde baked beans on toast/ microwaved potato – with grated

cheese for extra protein

4. Stir-fry - 69p from Tescos, takes 2 mins to cook *and* provides some of those essential 5-a-day vegetables

5. Pasta, with varying sauces rotated weekly

6. Tinned soup

7. Spag bol/Mac cheese

8. Microwaved potato, with assorted toppings (although these are often limited to grated cheese or tuna mayonnaise)

9. Roast chicken - cheap
   and nothing better to remind
   you of home

10. Microwave chips - great in
    a butty with ketchup

IN THE HOME

Student housing is unique. Students have a knack of living in some of the nicest and most expensive areas of the city, yet still manage to keep their homes looking as if they are fresh out of the slums.

The kitchen

The bin will be overflowing to the point where the mountains of rubbish surrounding it will hide the bin itself. The sink will be so blocked that the stagnant greasy water it houses will need to be siphoned out

of the kitchen window, and the floor
will be covered in spillages to the
extent that no single square inch will
be safe to tread on without shoes,
for fear of contracting the new
hybrid of infections that has mutated
there. The surfaces will be covered
with mould, and wildlife will be living
in the Tupperware cupboard. Then
to top it all off the flat will decide to
spontaneously flood.

The bedroom

An unnerving place, from the body-
shaped mark on the ceiling left by a

previous tenant, to having
to listen to your flatmates have
loud, uncensored, inconsiderate
sex through the thin walls, where
the orgasms always seem way
too prolonged.

The bathroom

A room haunted by suspicious stains,
remains of dead soaps, and that old
sock of which nobody is quite sure
who the owner is.

ACQUAINTANCES

These tend to vary from uni to uni, but this is a general list of those people who are important to students, should you believe them helpful in your hunt.

The lecturer

Apparently s/he contributes to the student's main education. A student avoids the lecturer whenever possible. These people tend to be classed as Intellectuals and have been at university even longer than the actual student.

The tutor/seminar leader

These tend to be postgrad students or PhD students. Students do not like them because they mark their essays and therefore have influence over their grade, even though they are only mere students like themselves.

The cleaner

Students eventually learn that if they want to get anywhere in life, they have to be nice to their cleaner. Students cannot clean for themselves, so this person

is the agent who keeps them from
living in squalor. NB. Cleaners like
to gossip. Use this.

The bar staff

Bar staff don't like students,
because they always want discounts
and get drunker than anybody else.
Students want to be chummy with
their bar staff because they like the
idea of being 'regulars'. The bar staff
see a lot of the students, but refuse
to learn their names.

The flatmate

The friend who's there to pick you up when you're in pieces, being sick, or being dumped by your significant other. The same person you can't stand because they never wash up or empty the bin, always pay their bills late and constantly leave toothpaste all over the sink. By the end of the year you will never want to see them again.

The parent

A very useful person, particularly when acting as a personal cash-

point machine and laundrette.
However unless the student wants
something specific out of the parent,
it is unlikely to make contact.

The token mature student

All courses have their handfuls of
mature students, who are more
likely to attend lectures than the
younguns, so are therefore useful to
scrounge lecture notes off. A clever
student will make friends with one.

The Fresher

These are *everywhere* and they are

Annoying. The most irritating type
are the ones who haven't yet got
out of the school mentality and are
generally unpleasant and immature.
Others haven't yet got used to the
new freedom with which they are
presented, and can be found puking
somewhere inconvenient on most
week nights.

STUDENT ISSUES

T.V. licences

University is probably the first time a student encounters a TV licence, and as this anomaly is so new to them, they think they don't need to pay them. This is why the TV licence people target students, and pester them non-stop until they do get a licence.

Landlords

All students (unless they live at home) will have to eventually deal

with this issue. No doubt they will
lose their deposits the first year
through sloppy inventory inspection
at the beginning of the lease.
Keeping the landlord happy is
important, as well as trying to
make him do the repairs that
he is obliged to do.

Plagiarism

No longer is it ok to copy a
sentence from your friend's
notes, or an article off the
Internet – everything, absolutely
everything, has to be referenced,

or you will be accused of plagiarism and kicked off the course.

Neighbours

It is important to keep up to date on this show, it is all people talk about and you will feel like you've missed out on an important part of your life if you don't watch it for even a day.

Sex

Where to get it, how to get it, how often you can get it. Not much else matters.

Money

Where to get it, how to get it, how often you can get it. You know you're a student when you judge the value of something by how many pints you'd be able to get for it, and know all student deals available to you by heart.

Exams

These begin as stressful, because they are harder than A-levels and seem to be a lot more work. Analysing how much work it is safe to do in order to pass the exam,

and still look cool for not
doing much work, is a time-
consuming task, as the balance
has to be perfect.

Procrastination

This is what you do to stop yourself
writing essays or studying for
exams... improving your skills of
watching TV, making origami swans,
seeing how many bottle-caps you
can flip into a bowl, etc.

Takeaways

It is very important to know where

the cheapest and most edible take-away food can be located nearest to your accommodation and favourite drinking establishment.

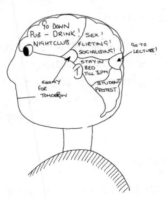

BREEDS OF STUDENT

This easy-to-use guide (in alphabetical order) should educate you on the most common and dangerous breeds of student, as uncovered by this researcher. Approach with caution if coming across any of the following.

BREED:
AMERICAN
VISITING STUDENT.

Name: McKenzie O'Brien
('I celebrate St. Patrick's
Day because my grandfather's
uncle's friend was one
12th Irish').

Gender: Female.

Age: 20.

University: Oxford Brookes
(because she thought it
was the same as Oxford
University), and Florida
State University.

Course: Completely
unimportant, she's only there
for a term.

Description: Stick-thin
(Beverly Hills slimming plan)

and likes to wear tight
T-shirts with patriotic
slogans such as 'I ♥ NYC'.
Is overly chirpy, and talks
excessively loudly.

Fav. Spare time activity:
Visiting quaint little
shops and bars.

Fav. Drink: 'Beer', the
American term for lager.

Fav. Food: Corn dogs and
twinkies, but she starves
because they don't sell
them over here.

Fav. Chat-up line: 'Oh my God…
I love your British accent!'

Natural habitat: Ye Olde

Touriste theme bar.

Is most likely to: be mugged by a bunch of xenophobic Bush-haters.

What is the point of University?: 'To get a British accent before I finish my English major.'

**BREED:
ART STUDENT.**

Name: Sylvia de Ste Croix.

Gender: Female.

Age: 19.

University: St. Martins, London.

Course: Art Foundation.

Description: Wears torn jeans and her t-shirt hanging off the shoulder. Must look scruffy but stylish at all times.

Fav. Spare time activity: Going to art gallery cafés (to be seen going in).

Fav. Drink: Absinthe (for inspiration).

Fav. Food: Sun-dried tomato, mozzarella, and basil panini.

Fav. Chat-up line: 'Will you be my life model?'

Natural habitat: The studio, where they smoke weed (for inspiration).

Is most likely to: win the Turner Prize for 'Bluetack on white painted wall'.

What is the point of University?: 'To be inspired by the intermingling of cultures and to develop oneself spiritually and artistically.'

BREED:
BITTER TORY-BOY.

Name: Terrence Banfield.

Gender: Male.

Age: 20.

University: Nottingham.

Course: Economics.

Description: Political aspirations and wannabe President of the Students Association.

Fav. Spare time activity: Runs the university Conservative Party society.

Fav. Drink: Cognac.

Fav. Food: Spotted Dick.

Fav. Chat-up line: 'I think you're divine, you have the

wit of my beloved Maggie,
and the mouth of Currie's
beloved Major.'

Natural habitat: Local
Conservative Headquarters.

Is most likely to: try and
convince you to vote Tory
within the first five minutes
of your meeting.

**What is the point of
University?:** 'University is a
government conspiracy. We take
out huge loans, get charged
interest, and then when we are
older pay more tax because we
are higher earners. Yep, it's
win/win for the Chancellor.'

BREED:
CHAMPAGNE SOCIALIST.

Name: Will Humphries.

Gender: Male.

Age: 18.

University: Glasgow.

Course: History and Politics.

Description: Supports the SNP, even though he is English.

Fav. Spare time activity: Smoking weed and muttering about capitalists with his friends.

Fav. Drink: Irn Bru.

Fav. Food: Potatoes, in sympathy with the oppressed Irish of the 1800s.

Fav. Chat-up line: 'My parents

own a castle, but I'm going to turn it into a commune.

Natural habitat: In a back-alley with his dealer. Really, for someone who wants to emancipate the working class, he does waste a lot of time and money sitting around doing nothing except getting high.

Is most likely to: show you his manifesto demanding liberation of the proletariat.

What is the point of University?: 'To reorganise the social structure of the world, man.'

BREED:
DRAMA STUDENT.

Name: Tallulah-Jane Q. S.
Darby-Goddard.

Gender: Female 'but I could
just as easily become male
whenever I am given the
impulse. I'm not pedantic
about my sexuality. It's not
becoming in an actor…'

Age: 23.

University: RADA.

Course: Acting, dahling.

Description: Ambiguous,
but resents being called
a 'lovvie'.

Fav. Spare time activity:
Reciting Shakespearean sonnets

on London streets.

Fav. Drink: Madeira.

Fav. Food: Cigarettes.

Fav. Chat-up line: 'I think we have a gorgeous connection.'

Natural habitat: Anywhere. I am very flexible.

Is most likely to: not give a damn what people may think about me as I'm an artiste and therefore, unique.

What is the point of University?: 'To immerse oneself in the profound mysteries of life. And to study Chekhov.'

**BREED:
ECO WARRIOR.**

Name: 'Stiggsy'.

Gender: Unknown. When does a man REALLY become a woman?

Age: 21.

University: Aberystwyth.

Course: Sociology and Social Anthropology.

Description: Protest whore, will hold up a placard against ANYTHING.

Fav. Spare time activity: Going to People and Planet meetings.

Fav. Drink: Fairtrade tea.

Fav. Food: Fairtrade chocolate (and of course

they are veggie).

Fav. Chat-up line: 'Do you know that there is an underwear-recycling bank just near my flat?'

Natural habitat: The forest amongst the peace-loving trees.

Is most likely to: tie him/herself to the nearest possible fence outside a G8 meeting.

What is the point of University?: 'To be part of the most powerful voice in the country, the student voice!'

BREED:
FOLK MUSICIAN.

Name: Eilidh NicDòmhnall.

Gender: Female.

Age: 22.

University: Edinburgh.

Course: Scottish Ethnology and Celtic studies.

Description: Plays fiddle, piano accordion, and melodeon. Grew up in Lewis,

Fav. Spare time activity: Playing in sessions in the pub (when not gigging).

Fav. Drink: Free ones.

Fav. Food: NOT haggis, trying to avoid clichés.

Fav. Chat-up line: 'Do you

want to fiddle with me?'

Natural habitat: The Croft in Lewis, or a smoky back room with a group of fellow folk musicians.

Is most likely to: be able to name at least 10 obscure folk musicians she has met personally, but who nobody else has heard of.

What is the point of University?: 'To live off a student loan for a few years without having to get a real job so I can learn more tunes.'

BREED:
GAY RIGHTS ACTIVIST.

Name: Andrea (but prefers Andy).

Gender: Female.

Age: 24.

University: Newcastle.

Course: Women's studies.

Description: Wears combat trousers and Doc Martins. Doesn't like bras but wears one just in case the occasion to whip it off and burn it in protest arises.

Fav. Spare time activity: Writing feminist poetry and discussing the Vagina Monologues.

Fav. Drink: Doesn't drink alcohol because it is a vehicle for the patriarchal society.

Fav. Food: Anything wholesome and vegan.

Fav. Chat-up line: Doesn't believe in them because they are demeaning to both men and women.

Natural habitat: Anywhere where she can rant about the patriarchal society using the family unit as a cruel social vehicle to keep the masses conforming to the heterosexual 'norm'.

Is most likely to: assume you are a homophobe until proven otherwise.

What is the point of University?: 'To meet similar-minded people, as coming from Wales it is tough being the only gay-rights activist in the village.'

BREED:
GEEK.

Name: Nigel Wood.

Gender: Male.

Age: 19 ¾.

University: Bath.

Course: Maths and Computing.

Description: Tall, lanky (due to malnourishment), and wears pebble-thick glasses. Favours unshapely jeans and T-shirts with slogans such as 'Dyslexia rules, KO'.

Fav. Spare time activity: Playing computer games, modifying and reprogramming his iPod to accept voice commands.

Fav. Drink: Coca Cola.

Fav. Food: 2 for 1 pizza.

Fav. Chat-up line: 'Did you know that L Casei Imunitass tops up your digestive system with friendly bacteria?'

Natural habitat: Internet chat-rooms.

Is most likely to: become hideously wealthy and get a stunning wife.

What is the point of University?: 'To get free Internet as long as you want. THAT'S RIGHT MUM, AS LONG AS I WANT!'

BREED:
HEALTH-FREAK.

Name: Jenny Legume.

Gender: Female.

Age: 20.

University: York.

Course: Geography.

Description: She gets up at 6:30 every morning to go on a four-mile run. Records daily calorie, carb and fat intake.

Fav. Spare time activity: An active member of the Capoeira society, Yoga society, Outdoor society…

Fav. Drink: Water.

Fav. Food: Organic spinach.

Fav. Chat-up line: 'You remind

me of my favourite Johnny
Wilkinson poster.'

Natural habitat:
The netball court.

Is most likely to:
become anorexic.

**What is the point of
University?:** 'To have plenty
of spare time to exercise
in, and to get away from the
unhealthy diet my parents
inflicted on me.'

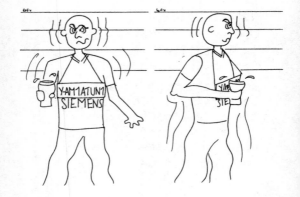

BREED:
LOCAL RESIDENT.

Name: Jimmy McKeown.

Gender: Male.

Age: 19.

University: Queen's, Belfast.

Course: Psychology.

Description: Lives at home. Anti-Catholic, anti-English, and anti-authority. Likes to get drunk and watch football.

Fav. Spare time activity: Getting drunk and watching football, pulling girls.

Fav. Drink: Anything in pint form.

Fav. Food: Kebabs.

Fav. Chat-up line: 'You're

dead on - I'll give you 10p to ring your ma and tell her you're not coming home, so I will.'

Natural habitat: The pub, duh.

Is most likely to: seduce a hapless 5th year, only to be too drunk to be able to 'perform'.

What is the point of University?: 'To get laid and totally wasted, mate!'

BREED:
MED STUDENT.

Name: Alice Li.

Gender: Female.

Age: 22.

University: Southampton.

Course: Medicine.

Description: From Hong Kong, speaks perfect English, and enjoys dissecting cadavers.

Fav. Spare time activity: Revising, feeding the ducks.

Fav. Drink: Flavoured soya milk and peach squash.

Fav. Food: Dried packeted seaweed and condensed milk sandwiches.

Fav. Chat-up line: 'Would you

like to join my study group?'

Natural habitat: Hospital library.

Is most likely to: become a consultant urologist.

What is the point of University?: 'To get a medical degree and become a brilliant doctor.'

BREED:
OXBRIDGE STUDENT.

Name: Julian Hargreaves.

Gender: Male.

Age: 19.

University: Oxford (Christchurch College).

Course: Law.

Description: Wears a scarf at all times, pink shirt with collar up, and deck shoes.

Fav. Spare time activity: Debating.

Fav. Drink: Pimms and lemonade.

Fav. Food: The Chicken Prosciutto served in Formal Hall is particularly exquisite.

Fav. Chat-up line: 'Look, my credit card has my father's name on it'.

Natural habitat: On the river, rowing.

Is most likely to: refer to his College at least once every five minutes.

What is the point of University?: For gents: 'To compete in a boat race every year.' For ladies: 'To marry someone rich and clever.' For both: 'To gather Contacts.'

**BREED:
OXBRIDGE REJECT.**

Name: Jonathan Hardwater.

Gender: Male.

Age: 19.

University: Durham (Hatfield College. Yes, we have colleges too).

Course: PPE.

Description: Lives to play Frisbee on nice days.

Fav. Spare time activity: Rowing, because it's not just Oxbridge that has long-standing tradition and a good river.

Fav. Drink: Champagne.

Fav. Food: Fois Gras.

Fav. Chat-up line: 'I play for the 1sts at rugger. Scored the winning try against Loughborough, don't-you-know.'

Natural habitat: Sitting in the common room bitching.

Is most likely to: try to become an Oxbridge lecturer and fail.

What is the point of University?: 'University is a class conspiracy, it bankrupts the middle class and gives those who don't attend the chance to earn money and get on the career ladder first, i.e. the working class.'

BREED:
PHD STUDENT.

Name: Adrian Lloyd.

Gender: Male.

Age: 24.

University: Birmingham.

Course: Biochemistry, PhD.

Description: Is only taking a PhD because it means an extra three years of being a student and he can't be bothered to get a real job.

Fav. Spare time activity: Marking essays from his seminar group.

Fav. Drink: Anything with caffeine in it.

Fav. Food: Anything microwaveable.

Fav. Chat-up line: 'I hold the power over your grade, now what are you going to do about it?'

Natural habitat: His office, *because he has one.*

Is most likely to: go bald and be using a Zimmer-frame before he ever gets out of uni.

What is the point of University?: 'To become a lecturer, and therefore never leave.'

BREED:
PRETENTIOUS
PHILOSOPHY STUDENT.

Name: Rodney (but he likes to call himself René for short).

Gender: Male.

Age: 19.

University: Kings College, London.

Course: Philosophy and Theology.

Description: Likes to wear scarves, tweed jackets, and write books.

Fav. Spare time activity: Sitting in arty cafés, smoking and having deep and meaningful discussions.

Fav. Drink: Coffee.

Fav. Food: Canapés.

Fav. Chat-up line: Quoting Plato.

Natural habitat: The depths of his mind.

Is most likely to: ask you if that's what you *really* mean.

What is the point of University?: Silly question. 'There is no point to university, it just is, like Bertrand Russell's universe.'

BREED:
RELIGIOUS
FUNDAMENTALIST.

Name: Nathaniel Godwin.

Gender: Male.

Age: 21.

University: St. Andrews.

Course: Divinity.

Description: Condemns the evil of liquor yet spends most of his free time in the pub drunkenly debating Catholic doctrine.

Fav. Spare time activity: Singing Kum-bah-yah and has a guitar with a rainbow strap.

Fav. Drink: Sherry.

Fav. Food: Tuna sandwiches (the modern day version of

bread and fish... Feeding the 5000, duh).

Fav. Chat-up line: 'The End is nigh! Give me your phone number so you can repent.'

Natural habitat: The CU.

Is most likely to: approach you outside the library and ask you if you have been saved.

What is the point of University?: 'To save as many souls as possible.'

BREED:
SPORTY JOCK TYPE.

Name: Brad Johnson.

Gender: Male.

Age: 19.

University: Loughborough.

Course: Sports Science.

Description: Likes to adjust himself in public, can usually be seen wearing a hoodie with an inane nickname across the back, and his rugby ball is signed by the England squad.

Fav. Spare time activity: Posing.

Fav. Drink: Lucozade.

Fav. Food: Weetabix and Mars bars.

Fav. Chat-up line: 'Don't worry, I don't do steroids.'

Natural habitat: The gym.

Is most likely to: ask you to feel his biceps.

What is the point of University?: 'To shag the entire (female) cross-country team.'

**BREED:
STRANGE INTELLECTUAL.**

Name: Unknown (possibly Tarquin, but nobody's bothered to find out).

Gender: Male.

Age: Probably 20.

University: Cambridge, but he doesn't like to brag.

Course: Anglo-Saxon, Norse and Celtic.

Description: The token erudite at house parties that claims to be trilingual, a professional salsa dancer, a Viking warrior, a shrew tamer…

Fav. Spare time activity: Running the student

radio station.

Fav. Drink: Caol Ila, single malt.

Fav. Food: Mushrooms of the psilocybin variety.

Fav. Chat-up line: 'Villtu heldr mínum brandi? Þat er mæri síðan ek þik sá' (Old Norse for 'will you hold my sword? It's heavier since I saw you.')

Natural habitat: Tórshavn (in the Faeroes).

Is most likely to: become addicted to coke and waste his life writing poetry about it.

What is the point of
University?: 'To unearth the
mysteries of the ancients.'

BREED:
YAH/RAH.

Name: Tamsin Highly-Robinson.

Gender: Female.

Age: 18.

University: UCL.

Course: English Lit. and History of Art.

Description: Wears Ugg boots, black tights, tiny denim skirts/belts, has shoulder-length, straightened highlighted hair, and a fake tan.

Fav. Spare time activity: Checking out cute law students and sussing out potential mates.

Fav. Drink: Smirnoff Ice.

Fav. Food:
Low-fat Caesar salad.

Fav. Chat-up line: None.
Men chat *her* up.

Natural habitat: Reading
Vogue in the café bar, or
Harvey Nicks.

Is most likely to: 'forget'
to turn up to lectures.

**What is the point of
University?:** 'To meet boys
and go clubbing.'

DISCLAIMER

This document is a work of fiction. Any resemblance of any part or parts of the document to real organisations or persons, or students, living or dead, is purely coincidental, and is in no way intended to infringe on copyright, trademark, or other legal rights of intellectual property, nor should it serve to distract a student from important studying.

This disclaimer is a work of fiction. Any resemblance of any part of parts of the disclaimer to real disclaimers, living or dead, is purely coincidental, and is in no way intended to infringe on copyright, trademark, or other legal rights of intellectual property.

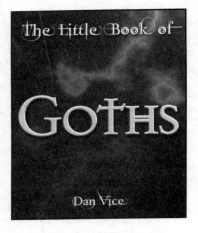

The Little Book of

GOTHS

Dan Vice

ISBN 1-905102-24-0

£2.99

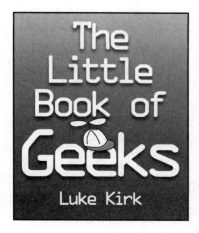

The Little Book of Geeks

Luke Kirk

ISBN 1-905102-27-5

£2.99

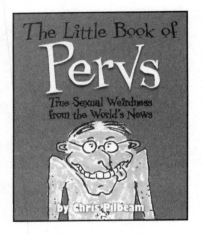

The Little Book of
Pervs
True Sexual Weirdness
from the World's News
by Chris Pilbeam

ISBN 1-905102-38-0
£2.99

THE LITTLE BOOK OF STUPID DRUNKS

A year's worth of real-life drunken mayhem from the world's news

CHRIS PILBEAM

ISBN 1-905102-23-2

£2.99

ISBN 1-905102-28-3

£2.99

All Crombie Jardine books are available from your High Street bookshops, Amazon, Littlehampton Book Services, or Bookpost (P.O.Box 29, Douglas, Isle of Man, IM99 1BQ. tel: 01624 677 237, email: bookshop@enterprise.net.

(Free postage and packing within the UK).

www.crombiejardine.com